AF480647

Orange Moments

A Journal of Grace in the Ordinary

This journal is a quiet space to notice the small
ways God meets you in the ordinary. Write
freely. Pause often. Let grace find you in the
simplest moments.

An orange moment is a small, unexpected
reminder that God is near — a whisper of
grace tucked inside an ordinary day.
It might be a color, a memory, a word, or
something as simple as an orange that catches
your heart at just the right time. These pages
are here to help you notice those moments
and hold them close.

Taste and see that the Lord is good.
Psalm 34:8